Helen Gibson Carves

The Animals of the Nativity

D1501331

Text written with and photography
by Douglas Congdon-Martin

Schiffer Publishing Ltd

77 Lower Valley Road, Atglen, PA 19310

Published by Schiffer Publishing, Ltd.
77 Lower Valley Road
Atglen, PA 19310
Please write for a free catalog.
This book may be purchased from the publisher.
Please include $2.95 postage.
Try your bookstore first.

We are interested in hearing from authors
with book ideas on related subjects.

Copyright © 1993 by Helen Gibson.
Library of Congress Catalog Number: 93-85231.

Printed in the United States of America.
ISBN: 0-88740-544-4

Contents

If you would like to know more about the history
of the Folk School and the Brasstown carvers, there
is an illustrated book available from the school.
Write: John C. Campbell Folk School, Brasstown,
North Carolina 28902.

Introduction

"So where are the animals?"

That was the question I kept hearing after *Carving the Nativity* was published. It was a good question. What is the nativity without cattle, lambs, donkeys, and camels? The problem was that they just wouldn't fit in the format of the book. But now it is a pleasure to bring them to you with the same, step-by-step illustrated instructions.

There are a lot of stories about the animals that were there the night Jesus was born. How they found their voices and talked. How they gave of their stall and of themselves as a gift to the newborn child. Their presence at the nativity remind us of the humble birth of this "King," and the mystery and joy of Christmas.

As I said in the last book, the carving of the nativity is a community project and tradition at the John C. Campbell Folk School. Hope Brown carves the standing angel, cherubs and the baby for the sets that are sold through the school. Martha Coffey carves the camels. Nolan Beavers carves some of the donkeys and oxen, and Ray Mann has made donkeys, sheep, oxen, and cows. I usually carve Mary and Joseph, the three shepherds, and the three wise men, so it was a challenge and a privilege to do the animals for this book. As always, I thank my colleagues and friends at the school for their support and encouragement.

We were pleased at the enthusiasm people showed for the first book. We hope that you will enjoy this book just as much, and that you will cherish the carvings of the nativity as much as we do.

Nativity Animal Patterns

THE STANDING CAMEL

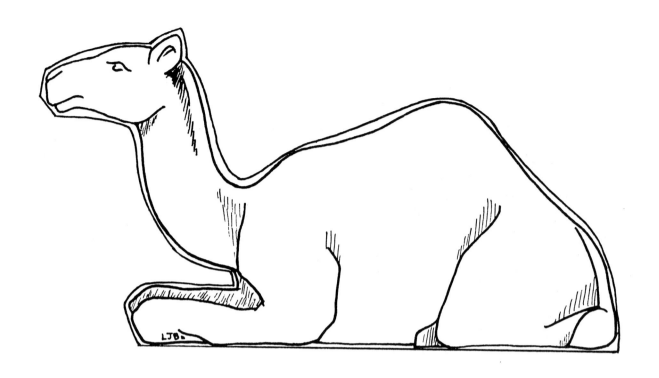

THE CAMEL AT REST

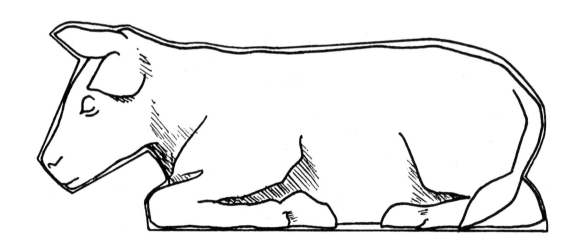

THE COW AT REST

THE STANDING DONKEY

THE DONKEY AT REST

THE STANDING SHEEP

THE SHEEP AT REST

Carving the Camel

Lay the pattern out on a two inch thick piece of bass wood and cut the camel out on a bandsaw.

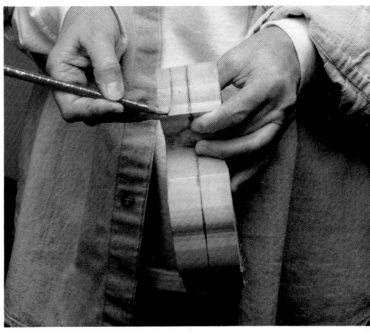

Divide the halves again on the head and neck, except at the ear where it flares out.

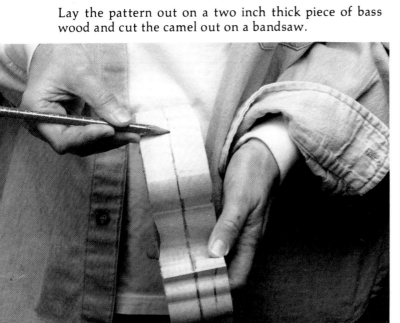

Draw the center line around the piece.

The lines drawn beneath...

and above.

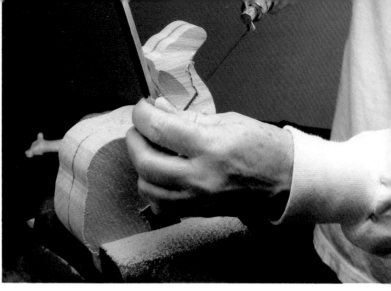

Do the same on the front.

Place the blank in a vise and cut the rough shape of the head and neck with a coping saw.

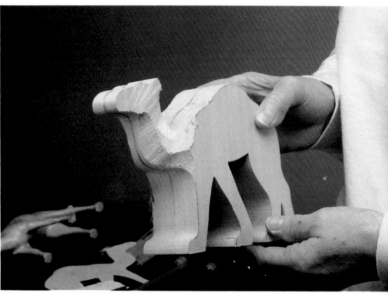

The neck roughed out.

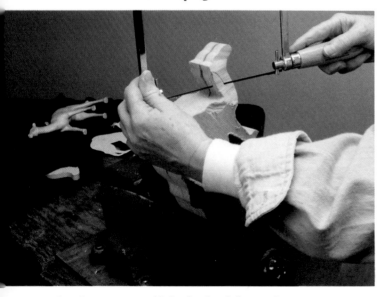

Take the corners off the back of the neck.

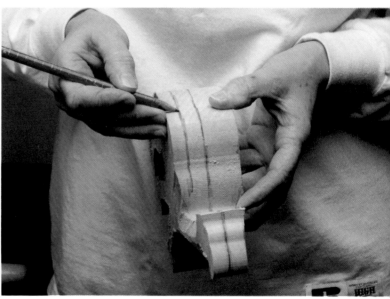

Along the back mark a line a little less than half way to center from each side.

Mark the sides a little bit thicker.

Turn the piece and use the same process on the front shoulders.

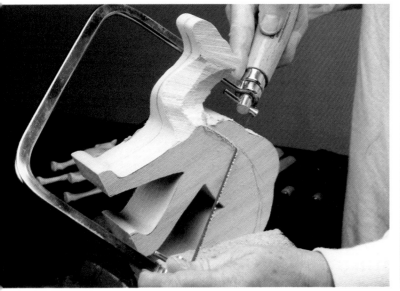

With the coping saw following both lines, cut off the corners of the back.

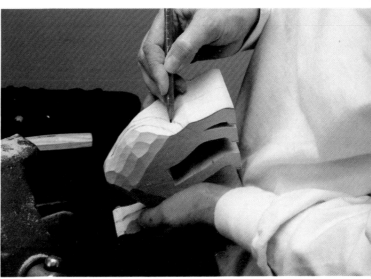

Draw in the tail.

Before cutting the legs, use a large gouge to shape the back. This allows you to use the vise. After the legs are cut they are too weak for the vise.

Draw the line of the feet on the bottom. They should be about two-thirds of the way from the outside to the center.

Do the other side.

With the piece in the vise, cut between the back legs. To avoid the front legs, angle the saw and the piece backwards.

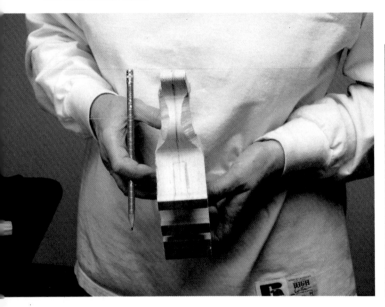

Bring the line up the front of the legs and square them off at the top creating the space between the legs.

You should end up with a nice wedge like this.

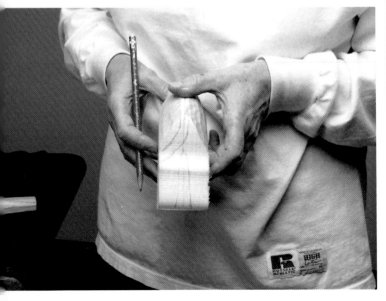

The back legs come together at a point.

Turn the piece around and do the front in the same way.

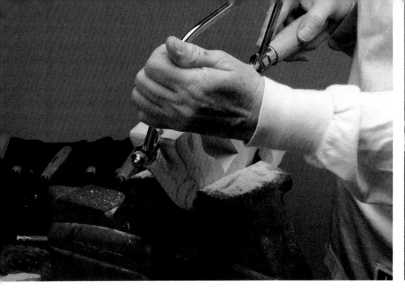

With the back legs done first, you have room to work.

Remove the marked legs. With some it will be easier to go from the toe...

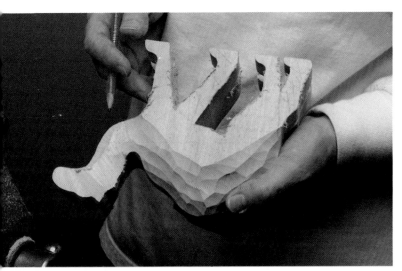

Right now you have eight legs. On the right side of the camel the legs toward the back will be marked for removal.

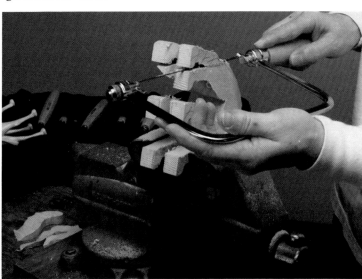

and with others it will be easier to go from the side.

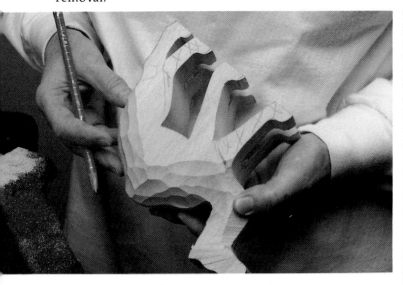

On the left side, the forward legs will be removed.

Do the front in the same way. Do one leg...

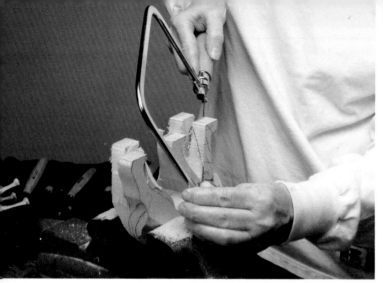

then the other.

You are left with nubs of legs.

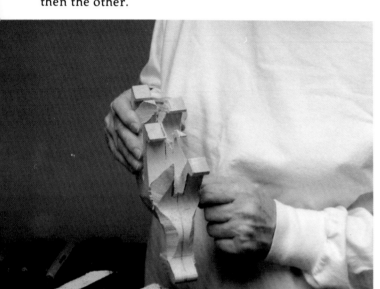

You are left with some wood between,

Chisel them away with a large gouge.

so you need to make the cut deeper now that you have access to it.

In the front, remove the legs and establish the line of the chest. You should do some shaping as you go.

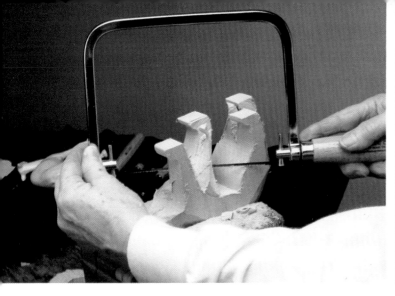

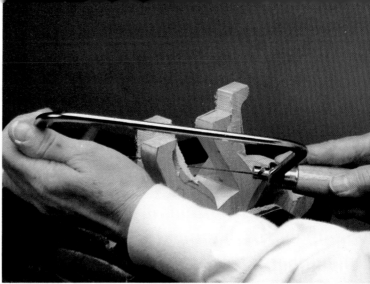

On this leg you can make the job easier by making several cuts with the coping saw....

Move to the back legs and remove as much as you can with the coping saw.

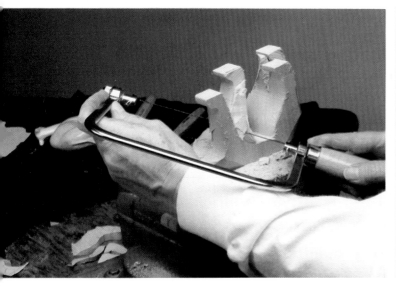

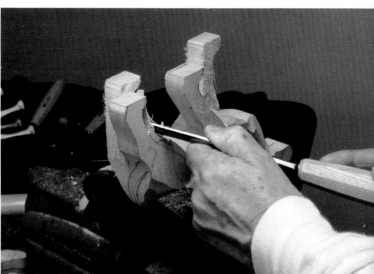

then come back at it from the side.

Trim it up with the gouge.

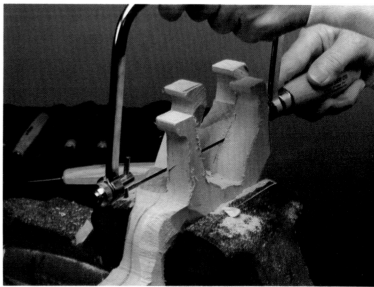

Clean up the work with a gouge.

Make the line between the back legs deeper with the coping saw.

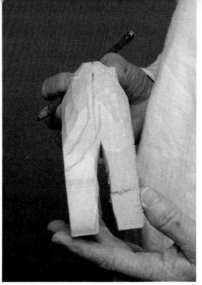

Trim back to it with the gouge.

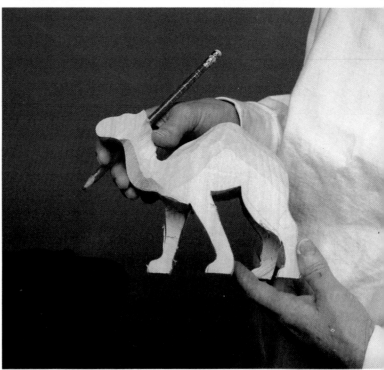

Come in from both sides, forming a v-shaped valley between the legs.

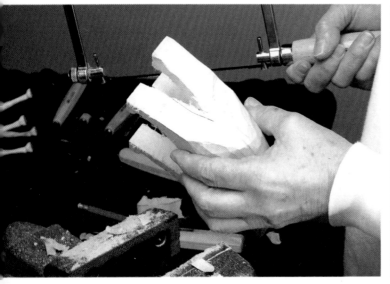

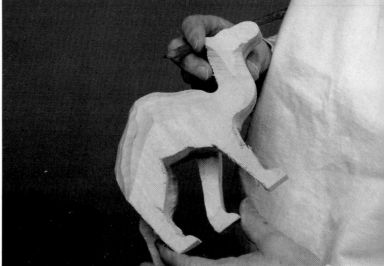

After the valley is established you can go back with your coping saw and continue the line of the leg up to the tail.

The saw and gouge work should take you to this point. We are now ready for the finer carving.

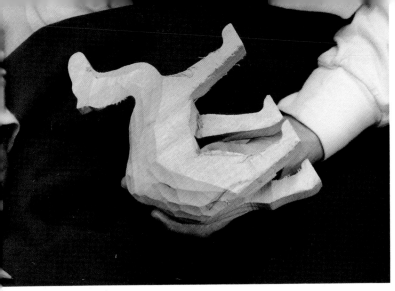

Mark the back leg on one side...

Smooth off the gouge marks.

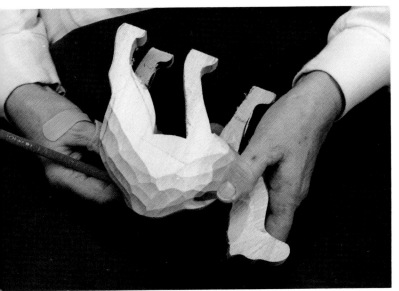

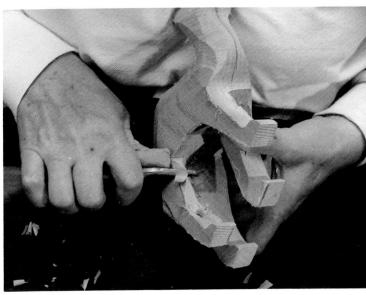

and the other.

Do the same thing on the other side.

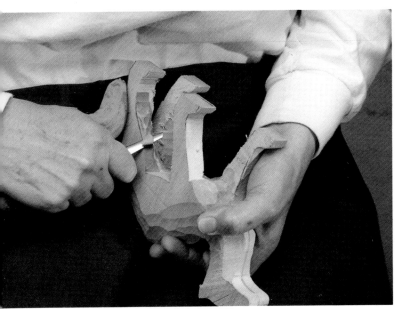

With a knife trim off the excess.

Make a stop cut around the tail.

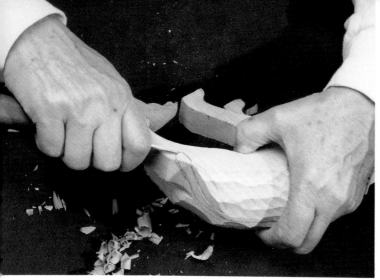

Continue to the tip.

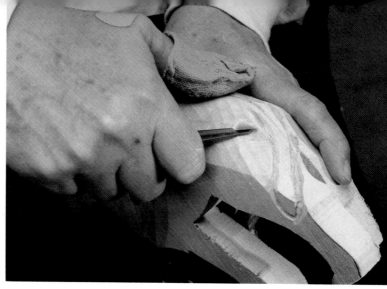

Shape the back of the hip.

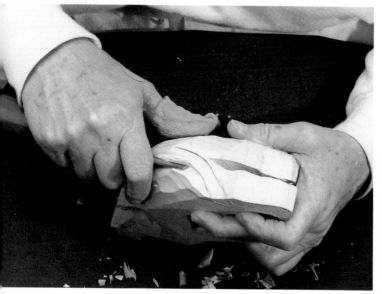

Trim back to the stop from the legs.

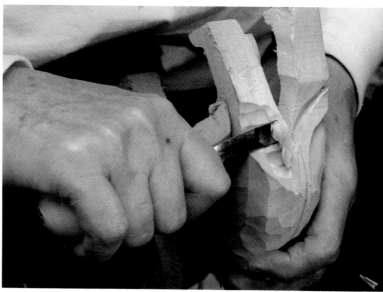

With a broader flatter gouge shape the back of the leg by cutting from the outside in.

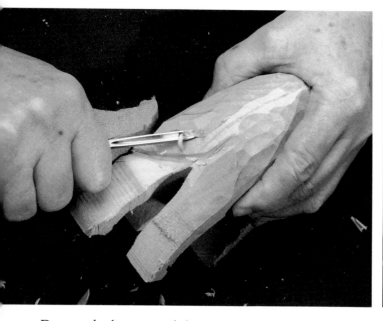

Deepen the line around the tail with a gouge.

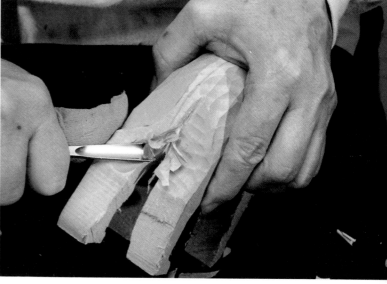

Do the same under the tail on the other leg.

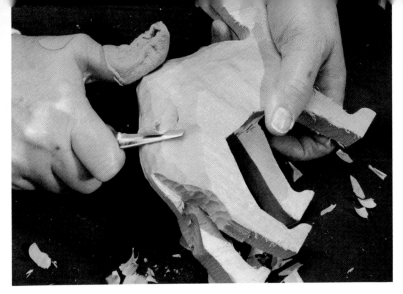

After the back legs are shaped go back with a knife and thin the body a little more.

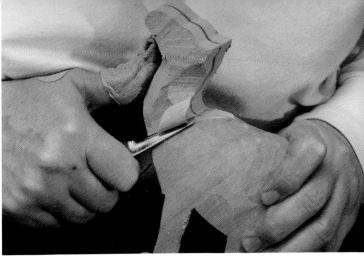

Thin the shoulders. The hips and the shoulders need to be thinner than the midsection of the camel.

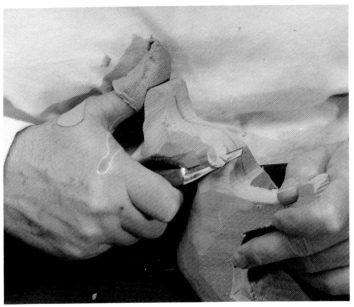

Under the jaw line, thin the neck.

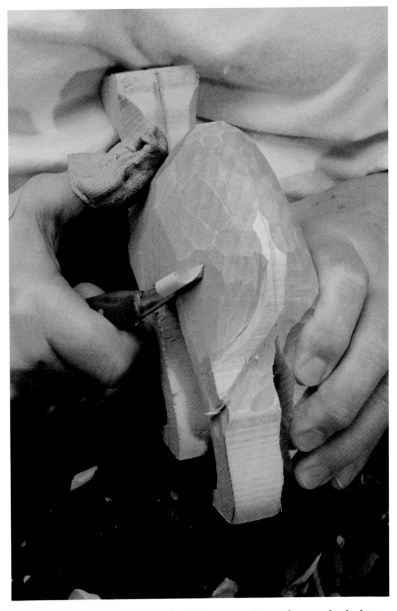

Come down on the back hips, making them a little bit concave.

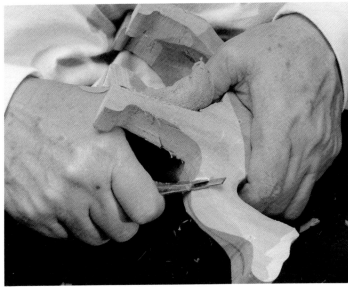

Continue to round off the corners of the neck, carving away saw marks and shaping as you go.

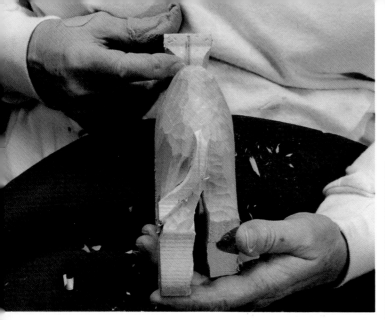

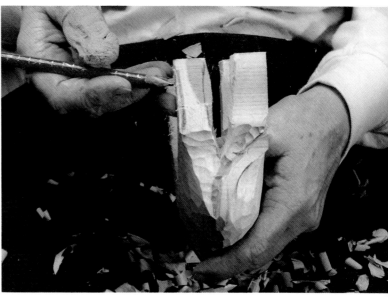

Mark the lower legs to be thinned.

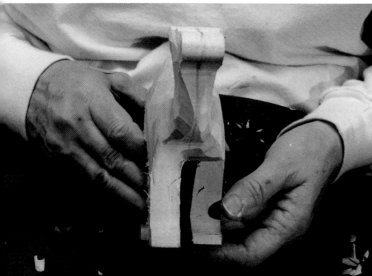

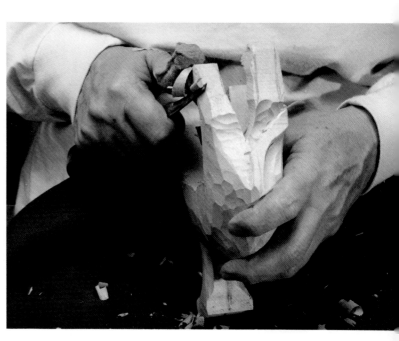

Trim the legs to size, keeping everything square for now.

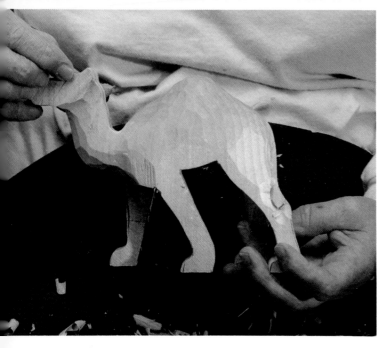

Progress on the body.

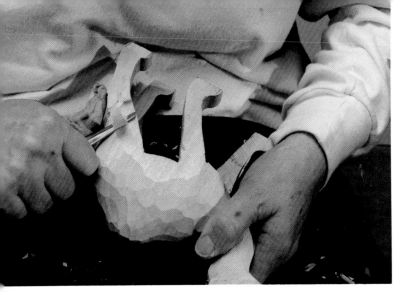

Trim the upper leg to match the lower.

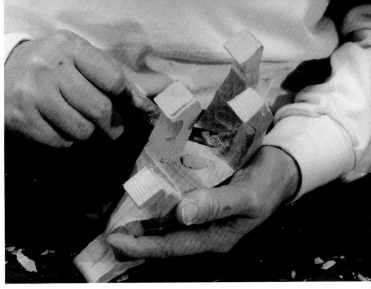

A gouge is useful to clean the hard to reach area inside the legs.

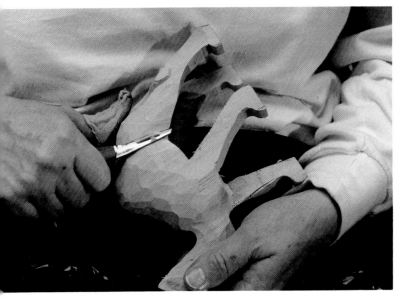

Shape the flank, creating the flow between the body and the upper leg.

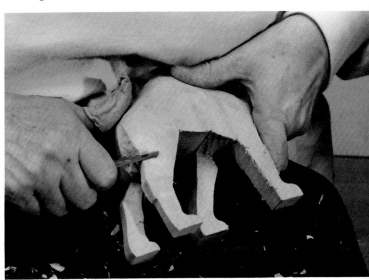

Repeat the process on the other side.

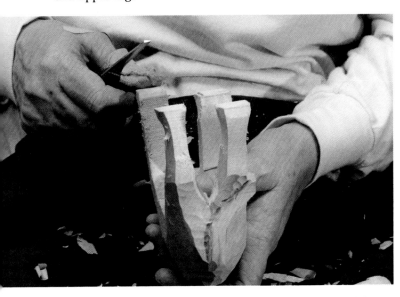

As you slim the legs be sure to leave enough wood for the camel's big feet.

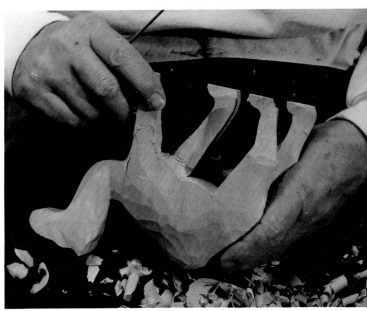

Cut a curve behind the foot at the heel.

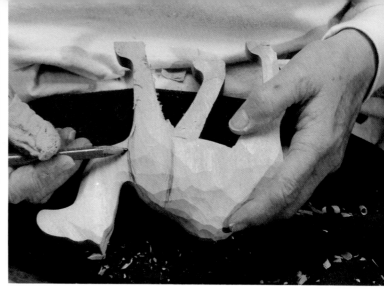

Draw in the lines on the shoulders on one side...

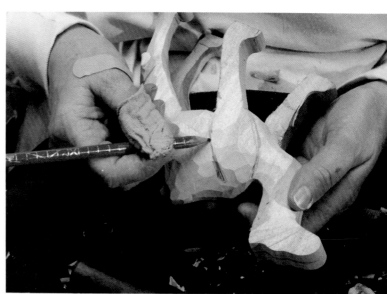

and the other.

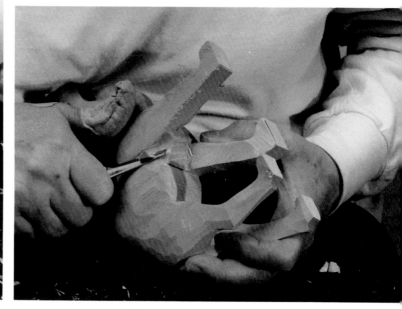

The back legs shaped to square.

Round off the belly behind the front leg.

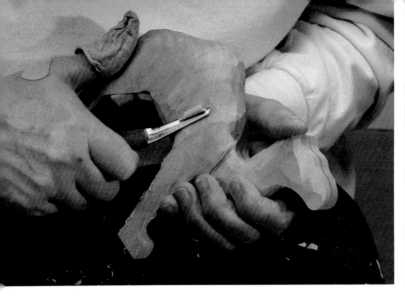

With your knife, dip in behind the shoulder to bring it out.

Mark the position of the front knees. They should be nearly level with the back knees.

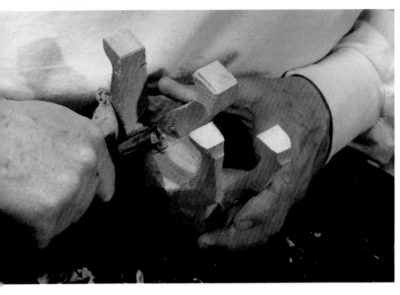

Use a gouge to clean up where the knife won't reach.

Start thinning the front legs, working from the knee down...

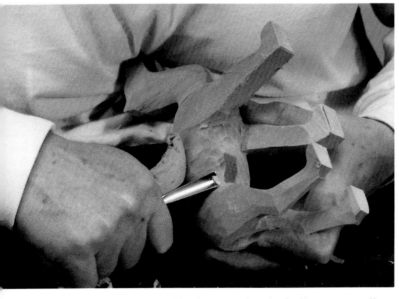

Going across grain, like here under the belly, it is usually easier to use a gouge.

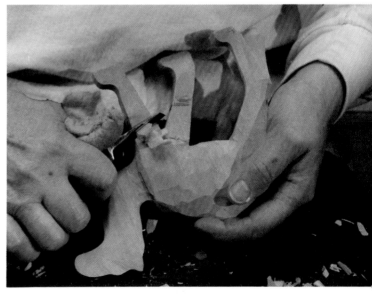

and from the knee up.

23

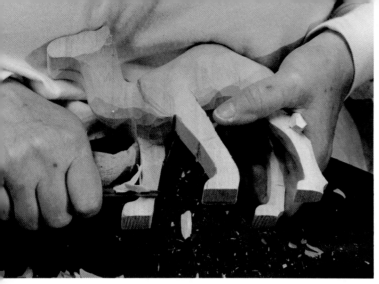

Do the same thing on the inside.

Cup out in front of the shoulder toward the neck.

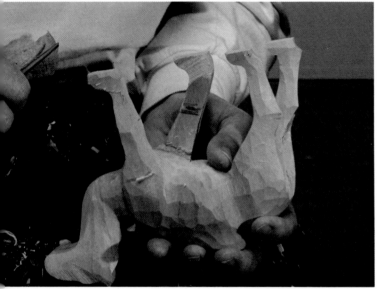

Cup the back of the foot, as you did on the back feet.

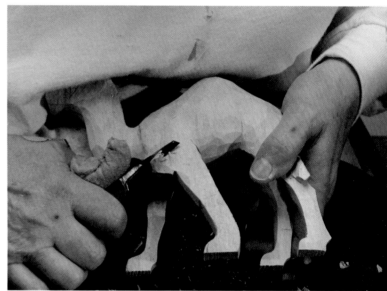

Do the other leg in the same way.

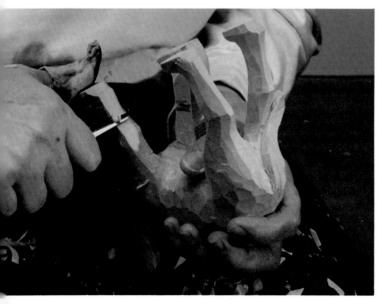

Trim the front and back of the leg in the same way as the sides.

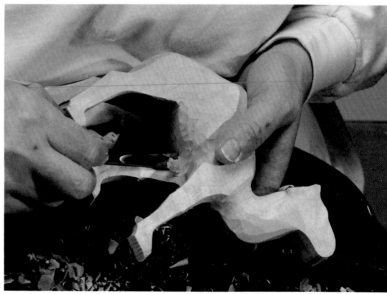

I can't get my knife on the inside of this leg, so I switched to a rather flat palm gouge.

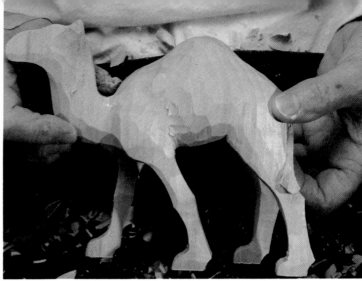

The grain here was running a little down and forward, making it difficult with the knife. I switch to a wide gouge, and shaping behind the shoulder is made easy.

To this point the legs, neck and head are taken to square. To get proportions correct, it is important to go to square before you begin to round things off.

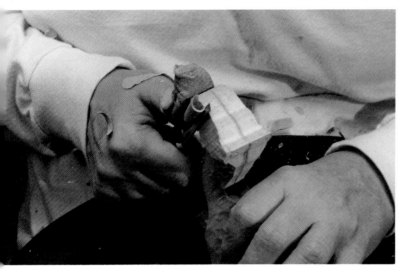

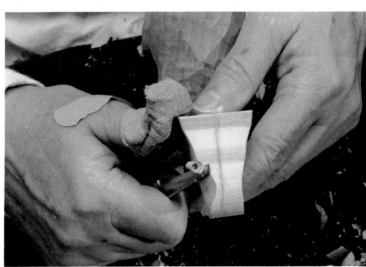

Working from the ears to the nose, flatten the sides of the head.

Knock off the corner of the muzzle back to the eye, leaving the eye wide.

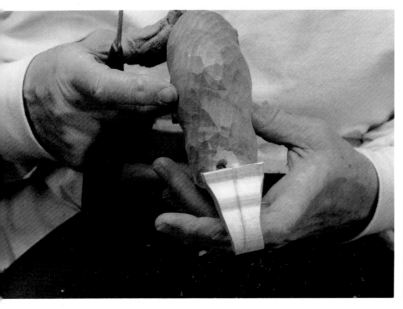

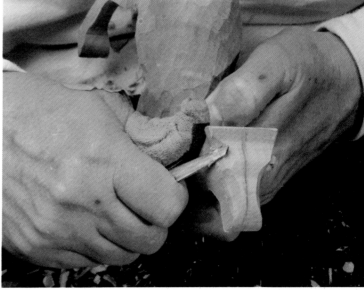

You want this kind of wedge shape.

Next knock the corner off from the eye to the ear.

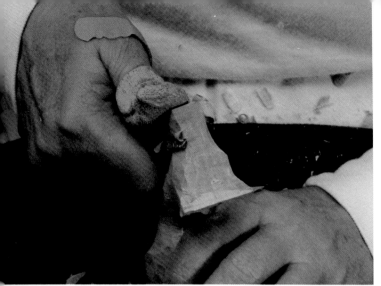

Thin the muzzle.

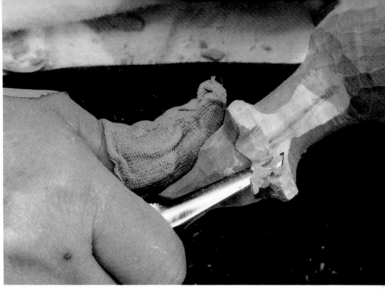

Chip that area out.

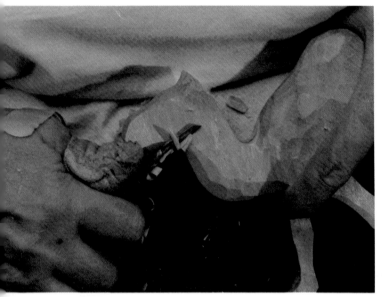

The eye area needs to be thicker than the jaw, so I need to trim down the jaw a little.

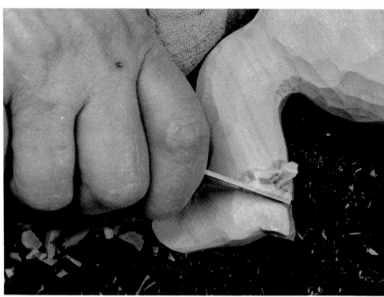

Define the back edge of the ear...

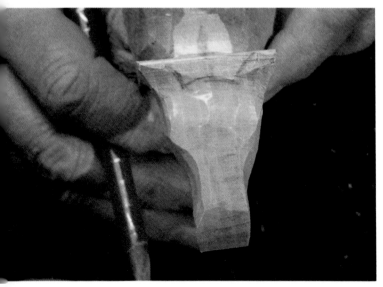

Draw lines to separate the ears.

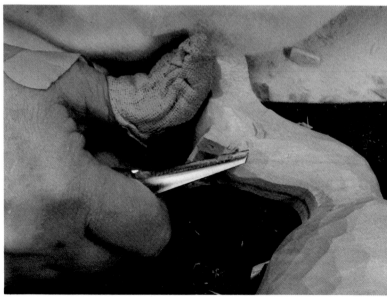

and trim back to it from the neck.

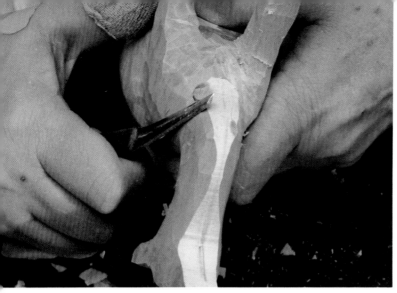

Thin and shape the sides of the neck.

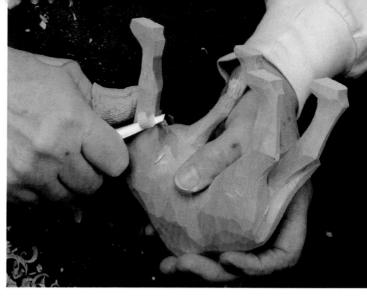

Knock the corners off the legs. After they are square it is pretty simple to take them to shape.

Like the feet, you need to get the head square before you start to round it off.

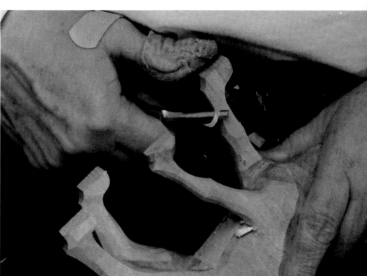

Do the same on the inside edges.

Now it is time to begin rounding up the edges.

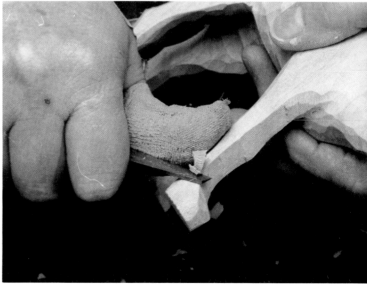

Round off the foot.

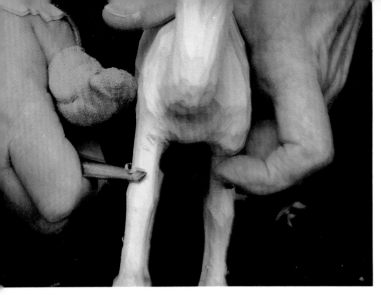

Work your way from the knee to avoid making it too small.

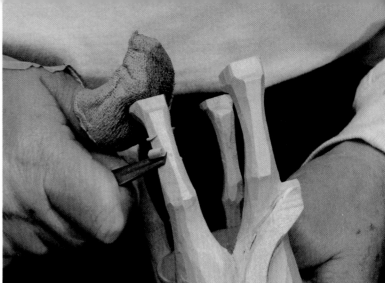

Round the back legs, by knocking off the corners.

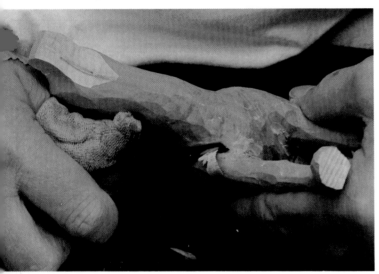

Shape the neck where it joins the leg.

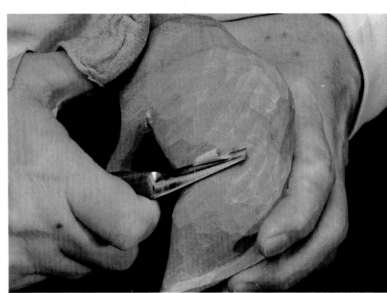

Go back and shape the flanks to blend with the legs.

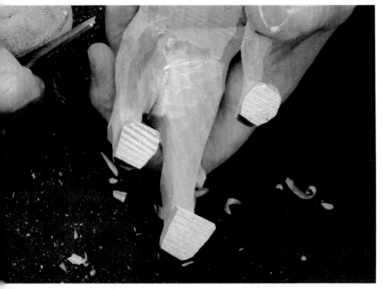

Shape the soles of the back feet, making them the same size as the front.

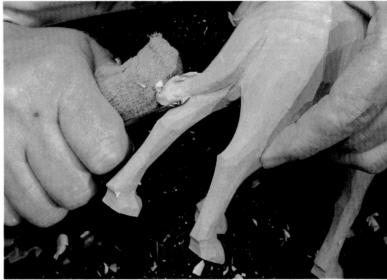

To avoid taking too much off in one space, move around the piece looking for places to round and shape.

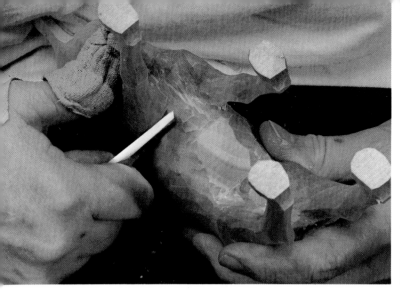

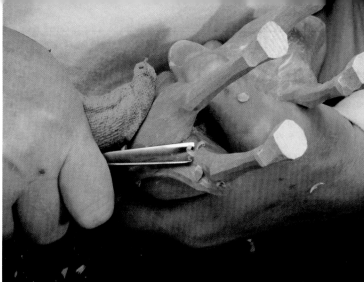

When the sharp edges are off, go back and clean up, looking for flaws and saw marks, like here on the belly.

As you work on the tail, you may find you need to make some adjustments to the legs.

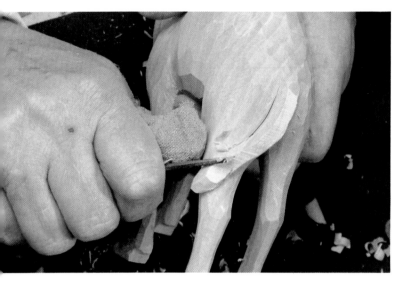

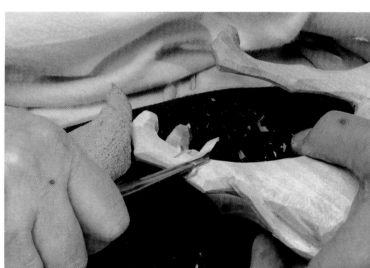

Trim up the tail, beginning at the end where we left it real thick.

Here one leg is a little thicker than the other and needs to be thinned.

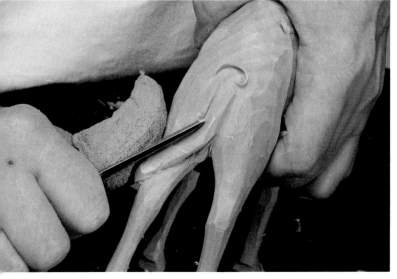

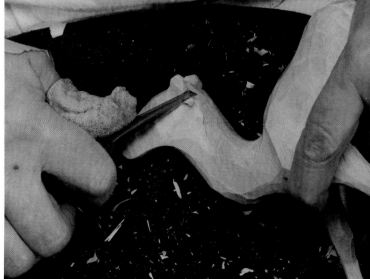

Thin the upper tail using a knife or a gouge to knock off the corners.

Define the line of bottom of the ear.

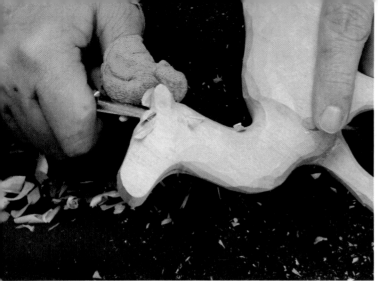

Shape the forehead.

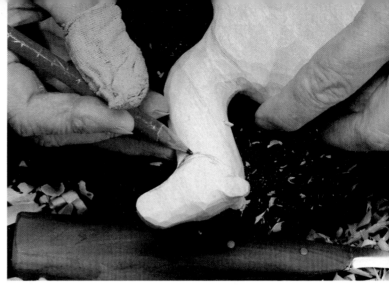

Draw in the jaw line.

Thin out the ears a little.

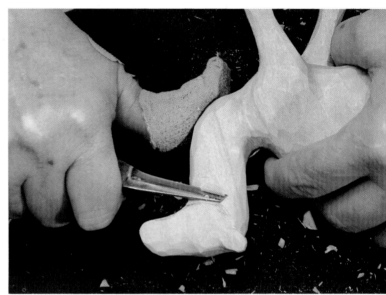

Starting at the jaw line, cup out into the neck.

Knock the corners off the muzzle.

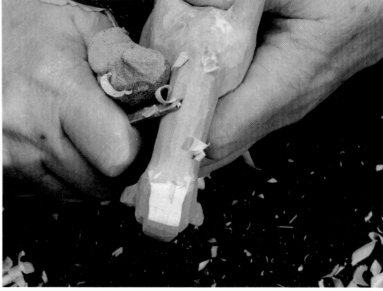

Shape the neck as you go.

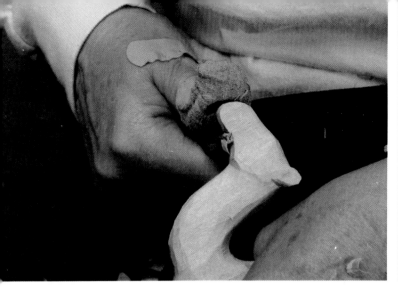

Knock off the under corner of the muzzle, but don't go too far forward.

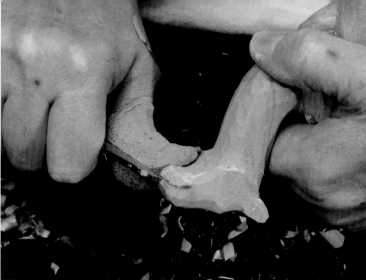

Cut a stop in the line.

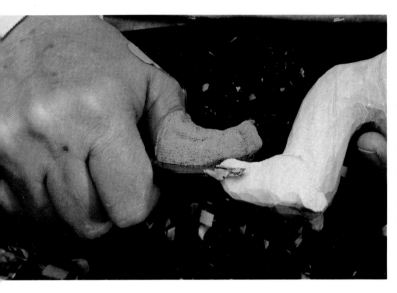

Knock off the corners at the front of the muzzle.

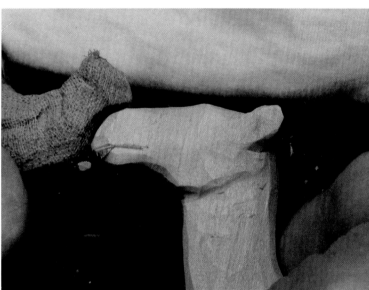

Trim back to it from the lower lip, making a v-line for the mouth.

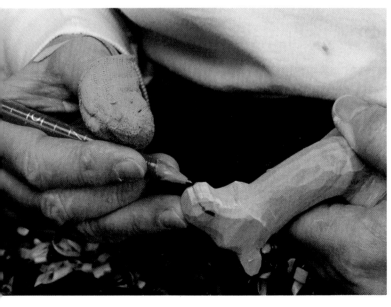

Mark the line of the mouth.

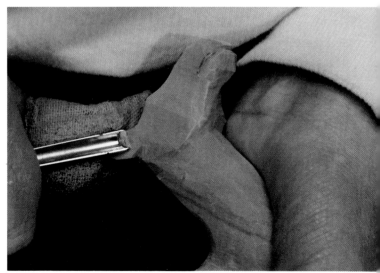

With a small gouge work from the tip of the ear to cup out the inside.

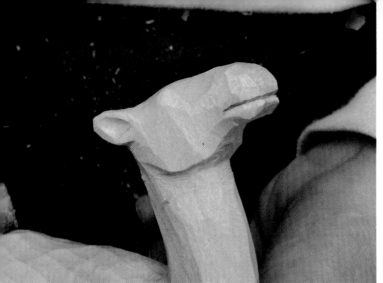

The result.

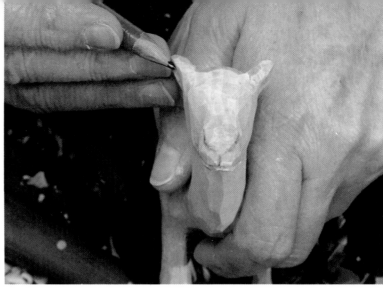

The nose area should look something like this.

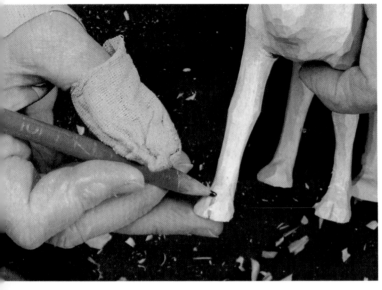

Mark the line of the cloven hoof in the front and back.

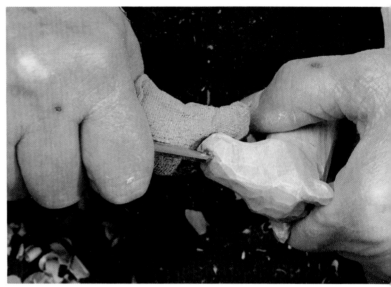

Make a stop cut for the nostril.

Mark the line of the nostrils.

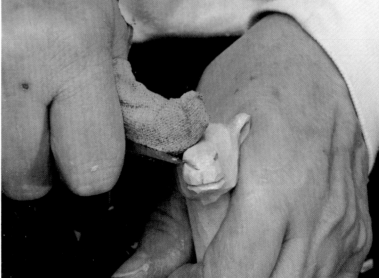

Turn the pieces and cut back into the stop cut to form the nostril.

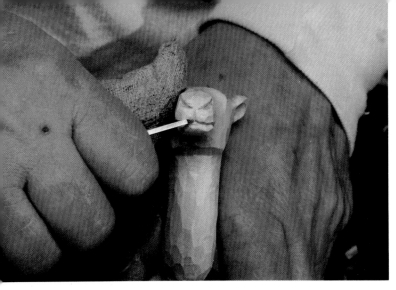

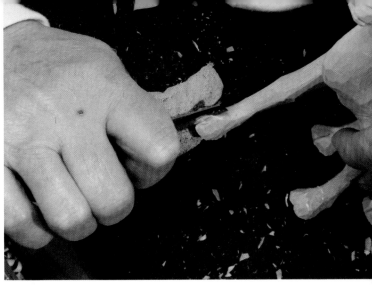

Cut the split between the lips.

then the other.

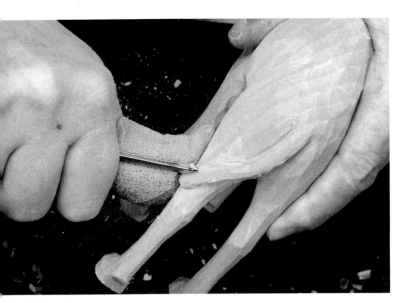

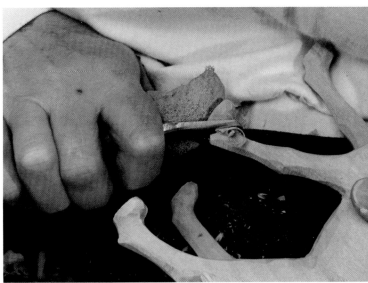

With a veiner, put the hair lines in the tail.

Continue to clean and shape as you see problems.

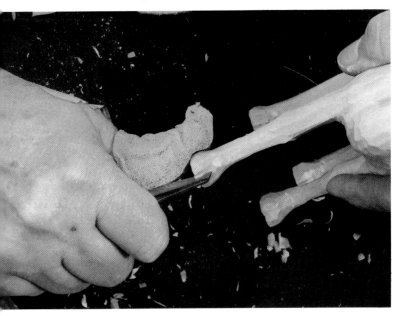

Cut the cloven hoofs first one way...

A round 6 inch rat-tail file will help shape and smooth the back and sides of the hooves.

It also helps bring out the ankle.

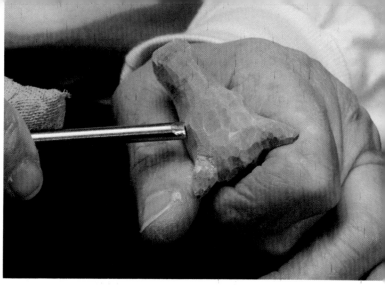

With the right side done first I can look head-on and align the eyes.

I use an oval eye punch for the eyes.

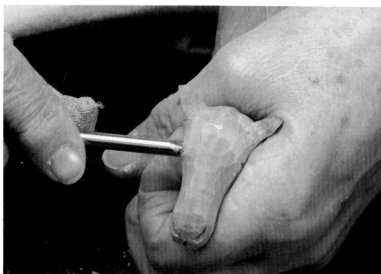

When the eyes are aligned and marked lightly, I go back and push and rock the punch to make a the line deeper.

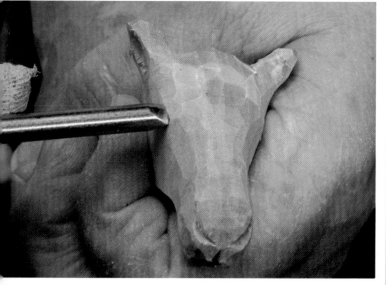

Mark eyes on the bulge in front of the ear then press lightly with eye-punch.

The result of the punch.

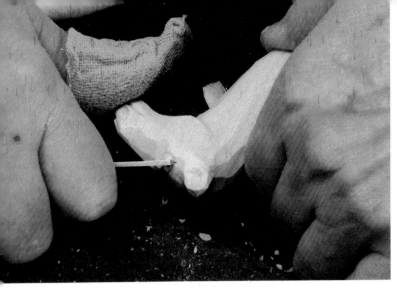

With you knife go back and deepen the corners. First cut one way...

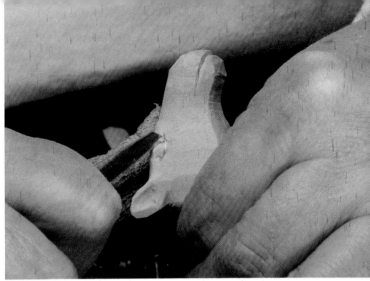

then the other.

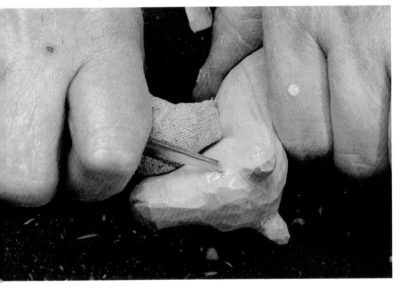

then the other.

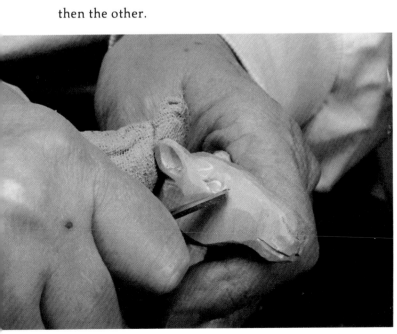

Do the same at the other corner. First one way...

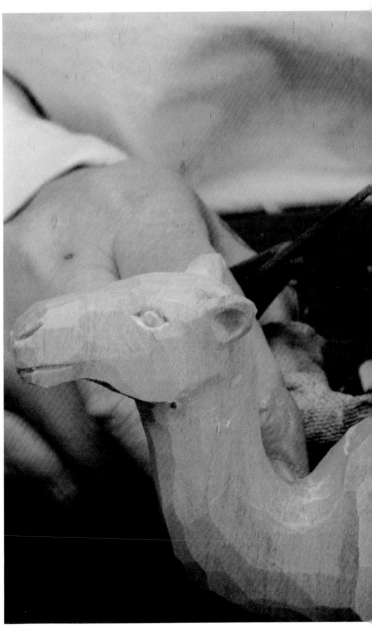

The finished eye.

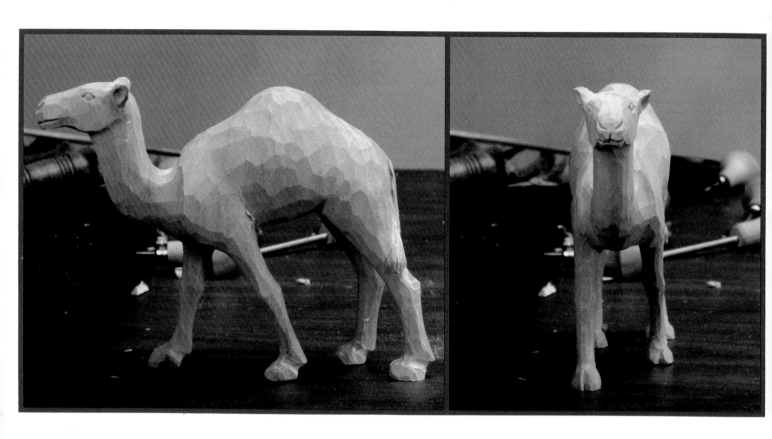

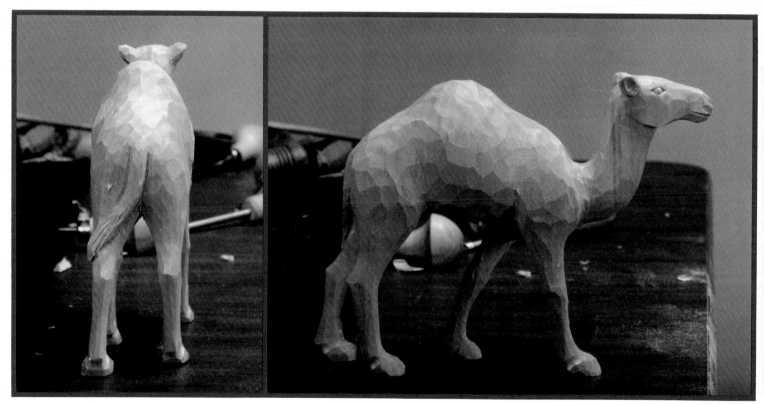

Ready for sanding.

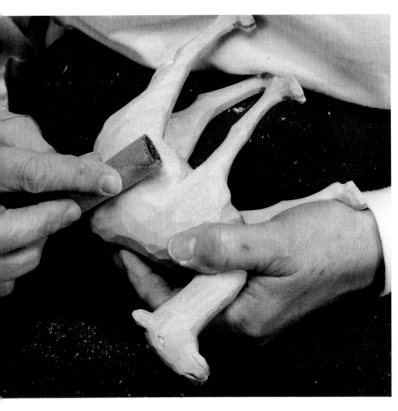

Begin sanding with a rolled up piece of 120 grit sandpaper. I use a cloth backed paper that I buy in rolls. With the cloth backing it lasts much longer. You can start anywhere, but I think I'll begin on the flank.

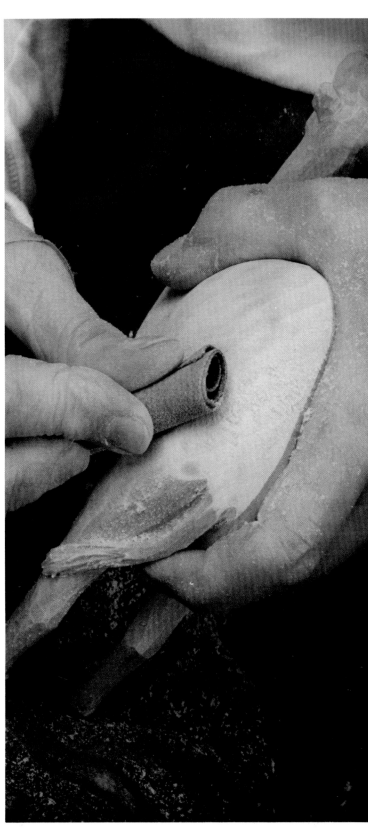

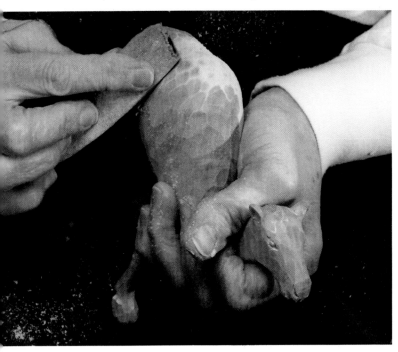

Continue over the hump.

As much as possible, sand with the grain.

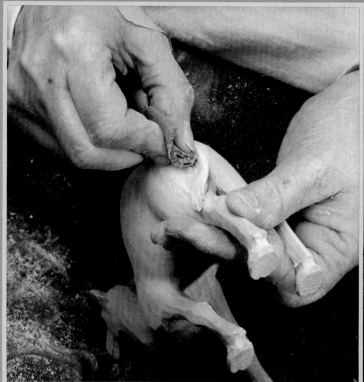

To get in the corners, flatten your roll of paper.

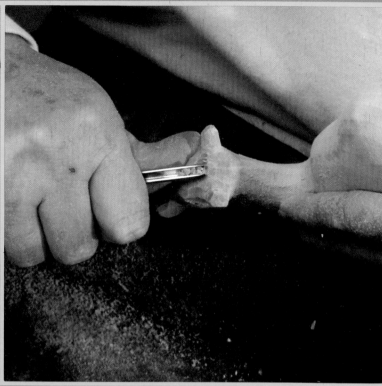

Before sanding the head I need to add a tuft of hair to the top of the head. I use the veiner for this.

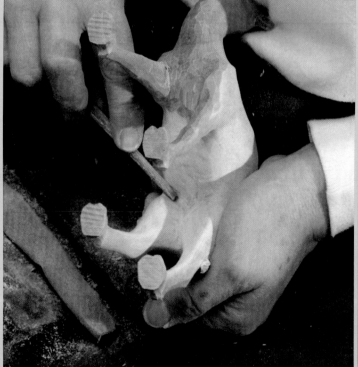

The rat-tail file also works in some hard to reach places.

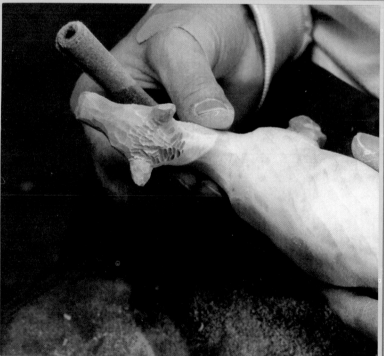

Bring this hair a little ways down the neck.

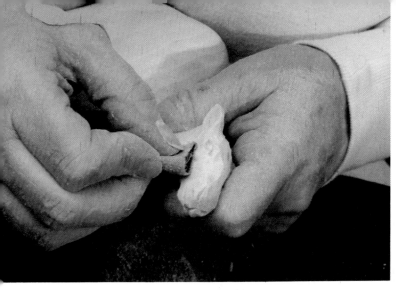

When sanding the face be careful not to sand off the detail of the nose and eye areas.

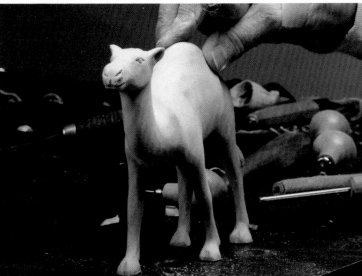

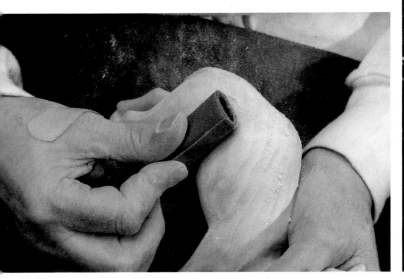

When you've sanded the whole camel with the 120 grit paper, go back over it with 220. This gives it a satiny finish.

Check the piece to see if it is standing level.

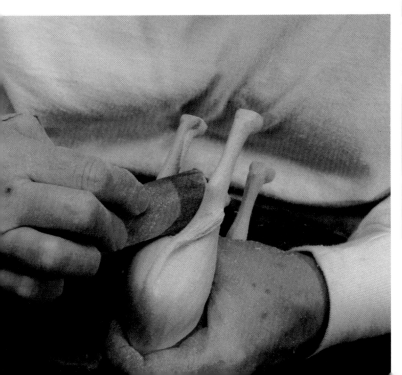

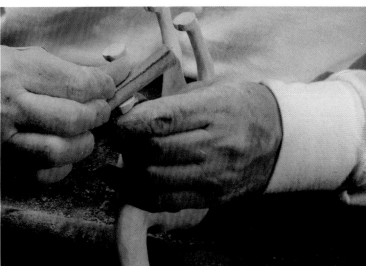

If its not quite flat, sand off the bottom of the two feet that are the longest. Repeat the process until the piece stands pat.

39

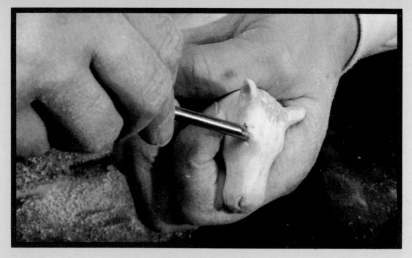

You may need to redefine the eyes and other details after sanding.

Ready for finishing.

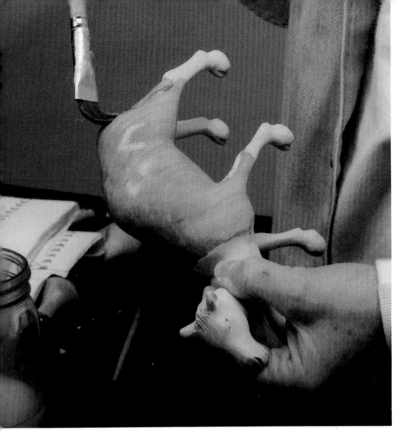

Apply a coat of Deft semi-gloss finish. If you can't find the Deft finish, we've also used a product called Hyrdocoat.

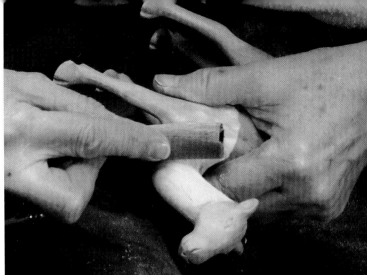

When the first coat is completely dry, give it a light sanding with 220 grit paper.

The first coat applied. Let it set aside for 45 minutes or so until it dries.

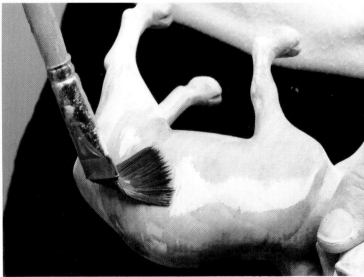

Apply the second coat.

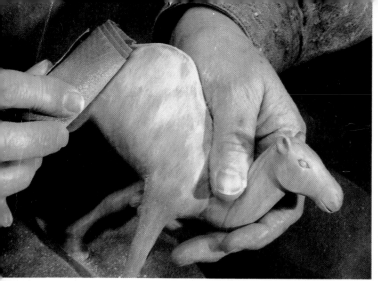

Apply a third coat.

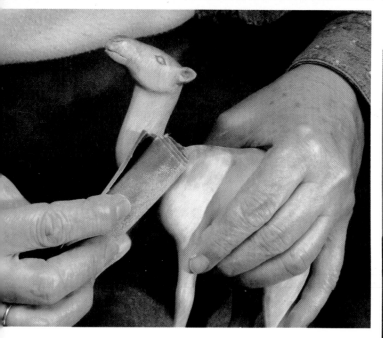

Sand again after the second coat.

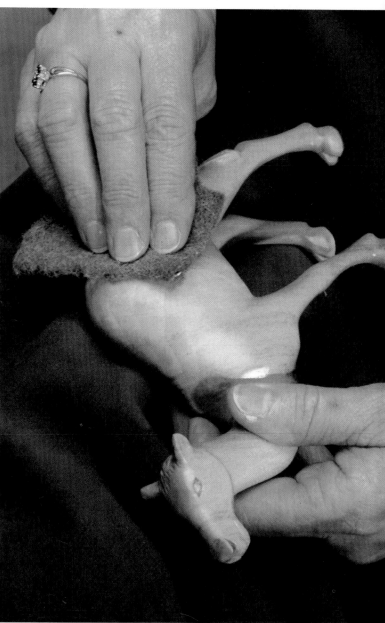

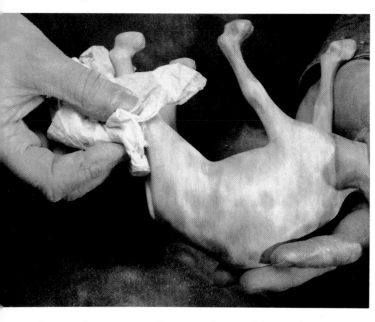

Remember to wipe the piece down after sanding.

Rub lightly with a ScotchBrite pad with no soap.

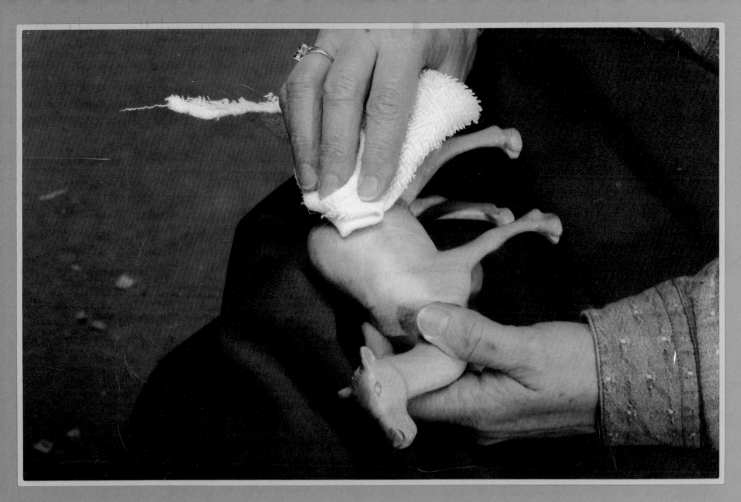

Apply a light coat of paste wax with a clean dry cloth.

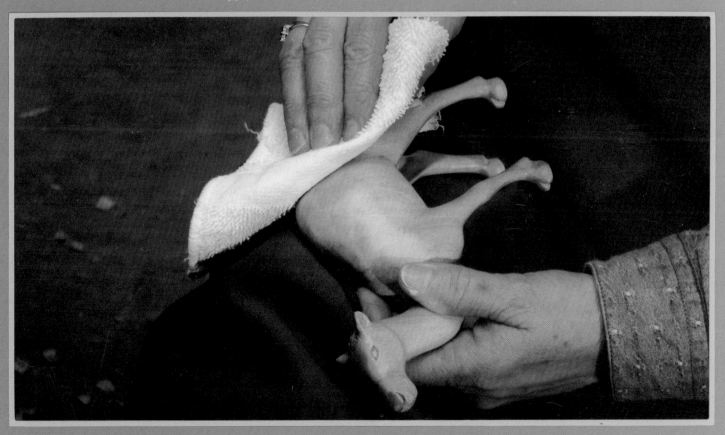

Buff with a clean cloth.

The finished camel.

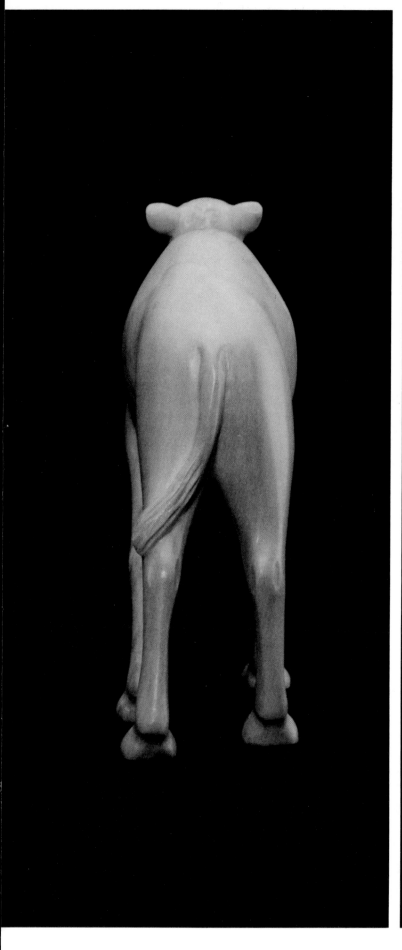

The Gallery